www.mascotbooks.com

The Story of Leaf

For more information, please contact:
Mascot Books
620 Herndon Parkway, Suite 320
Herndon, VA 20170
info@mascotbooks.com

Library of Congress Control Number: 2020921412

CPSIA Code: PRT0221A
ISBN-13: 978-1-64543-705-5

Printed in the United States

THE STORY OF LEAF

LAURA PACKER

ILLUSTRATED BY ARTEMIDA DEMIRI

FIRE

A FOREST FULL OF LIFE

Leaf took a deep breath, tilted upward, and smiled at Sun's warming visit. He loved watching the morning light glide down Mountain's slopes and slowly roll into the valley below, revealing its mosaic colors and winding river. Tree, Leaf's elevated home on Mountain's sunny side, gave him the perfect vantage point to watch Hawk dance with clouds, Raccoon fish in Stream, and Bighorn Sheep traverse rocks. He knew well the other leaves and animals who also shared his home on Tree, and found comfort in their easy chatter and steady activities. But he was most fond of Chickadee and Wren singing cheerful melodies about blue skies and open meadows. It was during these moments of lightness and joy that Leaf experienced true contentment high in Tree among all those he called friends.

Most days, Gentle Breeze would visit, sharing news from the surrounding forest: "Young Magpie is finally flying, Bear and Moose are still disputing, and Elder Deer has departed forest." When uplifting news was delivered, Tree hummed, sending strong vibrations along its branches into its leaves. But when somber information was shared, Tree momentarily held its breath, a stillness Leaf found discomforting.

For as long as Leaf could recall, he would hear advice and encouragement from a source emanating within himself. "Stay open and listen, Leaf," it would say, "for the world is woven within a tapestry of light and dark, beginnings and endings, and there is much for you to learn." This Inner Voice seemed to know a lot about everyday life, as well as the traditions and customs on Mountain—and certainly wasn't shy about sharing its knowledge. Leaf didn't understand everything Inner Voice said, but their conversations felt authentic and prompted him to think more thoughtfully about his surroundings. So Leaf trusted it, welcomed the guidance, and enjoyed his sunny summer days.

On one particularly arid afternoon Squirrel climbed Tree slowly. Head hanging low, he curled into a deep nook where trunk merged into branch, and sighed heavily.

"Are you all right?" Leaf asked.

"No," Squirrel barely whispered. "I don't understand what happened. Others chased me away when I neared their trees." He was confused and sad over the treatment, as he was only hoping to find new friends.

Leaf considered how difficult it would be to feel alone in a forest full of life. Unsure how to respond, he decided it would be best to simply sit in silence as a companion to Squirrel. "Will Squirrel stay sad for long?" Leaf conferred to Inner Voice.

"No, he will not," Inner Voice declared. "Emotions are flowing energy that strive for expression. They move through cycles like the seasons with beginnings and endings, for this is the way. Squirrel is young and doesn't fully understand these things yet, but if he is willing to listen, Mountain will readily offer comfort and clarity."

Leaf had received that same advice from Inner Voice before. While he had not heard Mountain speak, he was aware that Tree regularly found resilience and strength in Mountain's quiet and steady presence. Tree's roots were dug deeply into Earth, and its rings were wide with age, yet it always listened to and honored Mountain's wisdom.

As the afternoon heat intensified, Butterfly landed softly on Tree. Leaf happily provided shade and anticipated news about the valley below. Butterfly repeatedly flashed the iridescent yellow in his satiny wings, reminding Leaf of morning sunbeams shooting skyward over Mountain's crest.

When an audience had gathered, Butterfly recounted Eagle's grace as she soared high in Sky. "Her wings are magnificent," he said, mimicking Eagle gliding through the air. "But, of course, it is always wise for Mouse and Chipmunk not to stay and stare for too long." He described the vibrant beauty of Wildflower and of Hummingbird feathers, enticing Leaf to gaze down at the valley floor alive with color. Then Butterfly humorously explained Moose and Rabbit's preferred diets and Raccoon's attempt to cross the shallow part of river.

Leaf noticed how Butterfly's light-hearted stories created a lively atmosphere and brought delight to Tree's occupants. Even Squirrel appeared more relaxed, no doubt uplifted by shared enjoyment. Butterfly's visits passed quickly, however, and as he took flight with an airy laugh, Leaf found himself wishing these moments of friendship and ease would last longer.

"Be mindful, enjoy the present, and then let it go," Inner Voice said. "Wishing for things to remain the same will not bring you peace. It is not the way."

Leaf listened politely, but he could not help how he felt. Wasn't it natural to want to be happy?

EARTH

EARTH'S SONGS

As weeks passed, Wind brought periods of relief from the heat, giving Leaf the chance to dance and play on swaying branches. Occasionally, Thunder and Rain swept harshly across Mountain, driving Bird and Squirrel to find shelter within Tree's solid base and strong limbs. Forest news was regularly delivered by Breeze, Blue Jay, or Insect willing to stop and share.

Gradually, Leaf began to notice the days becoming a little shorter while the air around him felt heavy with moisture.

"Ahhh," Inner Voice pleasantly sighed. "Mother Earth grows thick with harvest. It is a bountiful time in the forest."

Leaf saw the animals around him satisfying their hunger with more available food and felt Tree sink contentedly into the rich soil below.

"Mountain continuously seeks to give and take in equal measures," Inner Voice explained. "Delight in this moment of giving, Leaf, for another transformation will soon be upon us, and the summer energy you readily embrace is passing."

Leaf detected some caution in Inner Voice's words and was about to question him further when Mother Robin landed nearby on Tree's limb.

"I have come to sing for Squirrel. News arrived that he might enjoy a song…or two."

Leaf smiled and understood Robin's visit and desire to soften Squirrel's hurt, for she was a notable elder and her charitable ways were respected in the forest. Robin perched on the outer limit of Tree's branch, allowing Sun's light to enhance the rich orange shades of her downy chest. Her melodies rose effortlessly into Sky, soaring beyond Tree's highest leaves. She sang of joy and sorrow, beginnings and endings, and how all situations in life come and go, like Breeze in Sky or Water in Stream.

Leaf noticed how the music vibrations seemed to lift him without the aid of Wind, inspiring an internal sense of expansion that felt incredibly light and free.

After the last notes floated away, Squirrel thanked Mother Robin for her musical gift. Leaf added, "Yes, thank you, Mother Robin. Your songs have uplifted all our spirits."

Mother Robin gently tilted her head and moved her attention from Squirrel to Leaf. "Those songs are not mine, little one, for they are much, much older than me. They have been remembered by Earth, shared by Mountain, and woven into Trees' rings. They are always around us, and you can hear them too if you choose to listen."

Inspired by Robin's words, Leaf set out with good intentions to listen for those ancient melodies embedded in rock and held sacredly by trees. "You must be quiet and patient," Inner Voice coached. "You are not well practiced at hearing deeply yet, but with time and effort, Earth's songs and messages will gladly reveal themselves to you."

Leaf's worthy attempts, however, were often interrupted. News of the forest, busy with activity, abounded. Sun hung lower in Sky, and Breeze's chillier visits urged the forest's occupants to build warmer shelters and gather provisions. The seasons were once again in transition. Another changing of the guard was in progress; an ancient ritual always respected on Mountain, never ignored.

Leaf watched in fascination and delight as a colorful scenery slowly began to emerge around him in striking yellows, fiery oranges, and vibrant reds. Magical in its display, Mountain's splendor was impressive.

"It's *so* beautiful," Leaf commented one sunny afternoon when a deep blue sky accentuated the rolling patchwork of radiant colors.

"Indeed, a lovely gift to us all," Inner Voice replied. "You, Leaf—you too are beautiful and worthy of inspiration, for you are not separate from Mountain."

Leaf had always felt a genuine sense of purpose playing his small role on Tree's branch, but he was neither grand nor revered like Mountain. Yet Inner Voice's last statement resonated within, and as he pondered his own connection to Mountain, he seemed to only have more questions. Inner Voice encouraged him once again to stay open and listen. Unsure whether that particular advice was working well or not, he decided to simply admire the picturesque surroundings instead.

METAL
LETTING GO

Leaf watched Tree become emptier and quieter as the other leaves around him drifted away, sometimes escorted by Wind or Rain, other times letting go with one big breath. Even Squirrel and Cardinal became too busy to visit and share news.

As each day gradually passed, a heaviness took root and increasingly darkened his mood. He no longer felt the enjoyment of dancing with Gentle Breeze, or the pleasure of listening to Bird's songs. And as the colors around him faded, Leaf felt something inside shift and sink.

"Something is wrong," he softly confided to Inner Voice. "My home is changing too quickly, and I'm feeling . . . strange."

"You are lonely, Leaf," Inner Voice said and gently consoled him. "You are grieving for what is no more. Look inward for the peace you seek."

But Leaf was not listening, and as his discomfort within grew more unsettling, he decided the time had come to take his own big breath. *Now I will be with my friends.* Anticipating the reunion below, Leaf inhaled deeply, let go, and watched his home slowly drift away.

Wind, however, had other plans and swooped Leaf up as he floated closer to Earth.

"No, no, Wind!" Leaf shouted. "I want to join my friends below!"

Wind did not listen.

"Stop Wind!" Leaf ordered.

Still, Wind did not listen.

Leaf tried to fight, diving for the ground in desperation. But Wind would not stop and carried him until Sky darkened. Sorrow overtook Leaf, and even Inner Voice seemed lost, unable to offer comfort.

"Please, please, Wind," he wept, "you've taken me too far away. I'll never get home now. Let me loose."

At last Wind slowed down and gently settled him on a large log. Exhausted from his exertion and drained by his loss, Leaf rested on Log and did not move.

Days passed, but Leaf did not move.

Rain fell, yet Leaf did not move.

Over time, Inner Voice returned softly humming favorite songs, enticing Leaf to join in. Nearby crickets and birds added soothing harmony, but it was the lovely, rich vibrations resonating just under him that finally stirred Leaf to move and look around.

"I am Mother Log," a kind voice stated. "Wind has rested you upon my back and you are welcome to stay as long as you like."

"Where am I?" Leaf asked.

"On the side of Mountain," she informed.

"Yes, but which side?"

"The side facing Great Lake."

"Oh," Leaf whispered.

Noticing his disappointment, Mother Log inquired, "Why are you sad little one? For Wind never makes mistakes when she carries her beloveds to new destinations."

With a heavy sigh, Leaf responded, "Because I'm on the dark and cold side of Mountain now, far away from my sunny home."

"Ahhh," Mother Log exhaled knowingly. "I think you've created an unfortunate story about your new location. Yes, Great Lake side tends to be darker and colder as you say, but Sun visits here daily, helps the plants around us grow, and always takes time to play with Deer and Sparrow. Tell me, Leaf, when you lived on the brighter, hotter side of Mountain, during those days when Sun burned for hours drying out soil and heating you up, did you not look forward to Cloud offering shade, or the arrival of darkness to cool you down?"

"Yeess," Leaf answered slowly, realizing at times he most definitely welcomed a respite from the intense heat that accompanied Sun.

"It is the natural way, Leaf," Mother Log continued, "an ongoing balance between light and dark, each different yet equally important, with a little of one always needed in the other. You have experienced the sunny side of Mountain and appreciated its gifts. Now it is time for you to learn about this side, for there is light and joy within the shade too."

Inner Voice strongly agreed, so Leaf thought it important to honor the *whole* forest and try to remain open to the messages it wished to share.

Over the next several weeks Mother Log thoughtfully introduced Leaf to the animals and insects she knew well, sharing her observations of their habits. She taught him Moon's songs of hope and courage, and lessons learned when she had stood upright and supported Hawk's nest.

Leaf settled into a new routine and felt cold air take hold, tightly wrapping itself around the forest occupants. "Mountain's energy is shifting inward," he stated one chilly morning, just after Frost retreated into the shadows. "It feels different than before, like a force deep within Earth is pulling me toward its center."

Mother Log remained silent, while Inner Voice gently noted, "Earth's energy is always flowing. Transformation is constant and a gift we all possess."

Leaf understood that forest held fast to its seasonal traditions, but he had found a new home on Mountain's dark side and wished to stay undisturbed in his current location. So without further comments, he quietly rested on Log's back, preferring instead to focus on the shades of white and gray that comprised the lumbering clouds above.

"Be ready!" Mother Log said urgently, interrupting Leaf's peaceful observations. "Brother Fox will quickly pass over me. As he does, grab onto the fur of his underbelly," she instructed. "You must join him in his warm den, for Snow is finally ready to visit Mountain."

"Yes, be ready!" Inner Voice echoed. "He arrives in moments!"

Doing as advised, with no time to think it through, Leaf caught Fox's fur as he slid across Mother Log. But as Leaf felt the distance between himself and Mother Log grow wider, a startled pang of loss suddenly seized him. *Wait, what am I doing?* Another separation was rapidly unfolding. At the very moment he considered letting go, hoping to convince Wind to return him to Mother Log, a strong vibration, rising directly from Mountain itself, carried a message of clarity and certainty straight into his being: "Hold tight, Leaf! All things are meant to change, as is the way. Have no fear. I am a part of you!"

So Leaf adjusted his grip and held on as Brother Fox skillfully moved through the forest he knew well, taking Leaf toward another unknown destination.

WATER

QUIET DARKNESS

After Fox stopped moving, Leaf finally let go and felt warm soil generously greet him. *This must be Fox's den.* As he looked around his new environment, dread slowly overwhelmed him. He no longer saw Sun or Moon, nor heard news from Tree delivered by Breeze. In fact, he couldn't see or hear much of anything. Distress quickly turned into panic and he was desperate to find a way out.

"Breeaathe," Inner Voice encouraged. "You are safe, and Mountain is here too."

Leaf thought back to Mountain's message. Surely he wasn't meant to remain in a quiet dark hole with stale air. If change *is* to happen, why must it always take him away from the companionship of his friends?

Leaf sighed deeply, for it seemed there was nothing else he could do. His thoughts eventually returned to Mother Log's gentle counsel. She would not want him to give up hope or feel sorry for himself. Instead, she would advise him to remain open and allow room for growth. *But this is so challenging. What lessons could I possibly learn in this dark isolation?*

Time passed. Leaf could not say how quickly. Without a clear view of Sky he could not watch Sun's path, or witness Moon's shape. He missed Mother Log's daily humming and the rustling sounds of Chipmunk looking for treats under dried plants.

When he felt especially lonely in the darkness he questioned Mountain's wisdom to *hold tight*. Yet, if he had remained on Log's back, he would be covered in layers of heavy snow and unable to visit with Sun. Knowing this didn't immediately raise Leaf's spirits, but a sense of acceptance began to grow, slowly unraveling his previous misgivings.

For a while, he watched Brother Fox come and go in silence, wondering if Gentle Breeze had visited him with forest news or if Mother Log was resting comfortably under Snow's cold blanket. Longing to know more about the events taking place beyond the den, Leaf could no longer restrain his curiosity and asked Fox for news.

Brother Fox knowingly smiled at this earnest request. "Of course, Leaf. I'm happy to share what I know. I was wondering when you'd finally ask." Fox laid down, allowing his tongue to hang slightly from his open mouth, and looked off into the shadows of his den. He spoke of the arrival of Snow, the deep winter sleep of Bear and River, and the beauty of Cardinal as she perched on Pine. He told tales of his own family's history, the excitement of chasing mice, and the difficulty of finding food during the cold season. "And yes, Leaf," he added with a sly grin, "Mother Log is fine, sends her greetings, and expresses confidence in your ability to settle in well."

As winter embraced Mountain, Brother Fox spent more time in his home, sharing animated stories. At times Leaf found himself laughing at Fox's witty observations or grieving along with him at the memory of lost loved ones.

Leaf developed a special fondness for Brother Fox and thanked him for his thoughtfulness and generosity. Inner Voice agreed and felt honored by Fox's willingness to share those sacred parts that tend to be held closer to one's heart.

"It is you who honors me," Fox replied, bowing his rusty orange head toward Leaf. "For my stories would hold no value if you were not here to listen and receive them with such openness. Time has arrived, however, for me to slow down, rest against Earth, and listen to Mountain's wisdom."

"What does that mean?" Leaf asked.

"You will soon see for yourself. Instead of my stories, listen now to Mountain, for there is ancient knowledge to be shared, which I too would like to receive."

Leaf followed Brother Fox's example and relaxed upon the shadowy soil beneath him. Listening to Fox's breathing, Leaf drifted into a dream-like state where images faded in and out. Messages arrived from Inner Voice that he could not quite make out, but knew were somehow important.

Leaf's own breathing gradually became deeper until it matched the flowing rhythm of Fox. A peace spread throughout the den, creating a space of stillness and safety that welcomed wisdom in to show the way. It was then that Leaf felt a soft nudge within his core, a gentle invitation from Mountain to look . . . to understand. The choice was Leaf's to make or not. He accepted.

There, within the quiet darkness, Mountain began to reveal its story. Time moved rapidly backwards as Mountain chronicled change after unyielding change on its angular slopes, within its shaded woods, and along its wide valley. Each scene propelled Leaf farther and farther into the past as he witnessed Mountain's life: centuries of days passing into nights, passing into days; of raging storms, long dry spells, and shifting soil; of animals coming and going generation after generation using Mountain for shelter, food, play, and comfort; of rivers and lakes rising higher and higher until Eagle could no longer see Mountain's peak; and of the constant outside transformation that never ceased.

"Look," Mountain urged, "Look deeper." And from a place of higher awareness, Leaf moved through the veil of exterior changes and peered upon Mountain's inner strength and resilience holding strong and true, never wavering or withdrawing—a steadfast force, glowing like

Earth's ancient embers, keeping Mountain grounded and connected to its core self, no matter what it was enduring on its outermost surface. "This is the way, Leaf."

Before Leaf could respond, more scenes swiftly unfolded of land covered in ice and water. Suddenly Leaf felt propelled higher and higher, leaving Earth far behind. Planets and stars filled his mind, another story much, much older than Mountain, now revealing itself: light and dark, joy and sorrow interwoven throughout all things, constantly seeking balance through beginnings and endings. The ageless laws of the Universe imprinted into the cosmic fabric, governing the rise and fall of constellations, the ebb and flow of tides, and the changing of seasons. An unending rhythmic flow entwined within the tapestry of all life.

Finally, one last scene, a gift to Leaf, revealing Inner Voice mingling among the stars, dancing on oceans' waves, standing still as Mountain, flowing steady with Wind, living in Tree as Leaf—as *him,* always connected to the world and cosmos beyond.

The time has come to let go, Leaf realized as a warm golden glow, reminiscent of Sun's morning visits, filled his entire core. *I see the world will continue to shift throughout millennia.. Even now, Mountain's surface is different from the day before. My inner strength and stillness are not dependent on my outside form, nor rooted in my location.*

Thus, with clarity and certainty that all things are meant to change, Leaf took a deep breath and allowed the fibers and cells that held him together to unravel and dissolve onto the warm floor of Fox's den. Another ending to make way for a new beginning. Now with all forms and shapes possible, Leaf understood the power of change and no longer felt afraid, for he could create a new life with a new purpose.

After thoughtful consideration, Leaf shared his desires, "I would like to understand shapeless freedom. To travel unrestrained like Wind and gather insights from many locations."

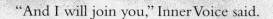

"And I will join you," Inner Voice said.

"Of course you will," Leaf replied with complete confidence. For he now understood that Inner Voice was never separate or outside of him. Nor was Mountain or even the stars above. They were all interconnected, continuously gathering and sharing wisdom, no matter the current incarnation.

Feeling liberated, Leaf released his outside form, wrapped himself into the luminous energy of endless beginnings, and transformed into a new essence: Water.

Leaf, now Water, affectionately whispered to resting Fox, "Be well, Brother, for this is not goodbye. We shall meet again, as is the way."

Water then sank below Earth's surface and headed for yet another unknown destination. This time, however, he was neither sad nor frightened of the idea of change. Instead, he tapped into the ancient energy that resided within all things, a knowledge that he too possessed the same inner strength and resilience and could connect with it at any time.

As Inner Voice encouraged him onward, Water listened to the sounds and songs that echoed deep within Earth. Beautiful and soothing in their own way, they were filled with those old, yet familiar lyrics of joy and sorrow, light and dark. He delighted in meeting Worm and Mole, and gained insights from the long memories of Limestone and Clay. Each encounter was an opportunity to learn about Earth's continual transformation and the important role of Fire and Flood in the ongoing cycle of beginnings and endings.

It was Great Lake that eventually greeted him with robust warmth and mirth, as if their reunion had been eagerly anticipated for months. Great Lake fully understood the power of change, for it had been living alongside Mountain for eons, undergoing countless shapes and forms. Experiencing a sense of belonging, Water decided to stay awhile within its vast and quiet pool.

WOOD
ENDINGS BECOME BEGINNINGS

One morning, as Water and Sun played together, reflecting light and colors off of Lake's glassy surface, Inner Voice spoke with conviction. "There is much beauty here, but it is time to continue on our journey." Water understood, for he too had been experiencing an impulse to keep moving.

Great Lake kindly confirmed this sentiment. "Our time together has been well spent, but Stream awaits your arrival. She is eager to assist with your ongoing travels."

After expressing gratitude for his period of respite, Water joined Stream and quickly slipped farther away from Great Lake's peaceful reservoir, though not before hearing the promise, "We shall meet again, as is the way."

Water flowed easily with Stream as she enthusiastically shared news of the forest. Winter had grown tired, making way for spring to take its place. Turtle and Wood Frog were once again visiting streams and ponds, while Oriole and Heron were seen returning to Sky.

Stream's obvious excitement was contagious, and Water could not help but feel enlivened too. Mountain's energy, which previously turned inward, had silently gathered strength and was now ready to burst outward, driven by Earth's eagerness to create.

After navigating through a particular lively section with Stream, Water moved to a calmer area along the bank and felt strongly drawn toward another direction. Inner Voice agreed that he was not meant to travel the miles ahead and urged him to follow his instincts.

"Of course!" Stream sang cheerfully after hearing Water's intent.

Thus, with a light heart, Water once again sank into Earth, but this time with a clear destination guiding him forward. He moved assuredly toward his goal, neither stopping to gather news nor listen to songs. Another beginning was beckoning.

"I have made a decision to exist simultaneously above and below, to gather news from Breeze and Soil, and to be nurtured by both the light and dark." Water then found the roots he was seeking and rushed upward, filling out trunk and extending along branches until he was fully absorbed and integrated into every cell, becoming: Tree.

"It seems you are enjoying your ability to change—and rather quickly I might add," Inner Voice jested.

Tree amiably agreed and laughed at himself, knowing shapes and names, like Leaf and Water, were always meant to be fluid, never fixed or frozen in time. He appreciated the guidance and ongoing dialogue his Inner Voice continued to share, no matter his present form. That voice within, linked harmoniously to his own thoughts and the wisdom of the world beyond, was and would always be a part of him—a sacred connection, safe and true, that he could rely on time and time again.

Tree then acknowledged and rejoiced in his current transformation. Vitality tickled his core as life around him began to wake up and be heard. Bright green buds on his branches took big breaths and became rounded, fresh leaves. Eager to take in Sun's energy, Tree expanded outward and welcomed all those who chose to call him home.

Tree felt responsible for nurturing the habitat that he now provided to many lifeforms. He reverently recalled Mother Log's stories of the time she stood tall and the lessons she had learned.

"Thank you for the knowledge you shared with me," he whispered, knowing Wind would carry his message not only to Mother Log, but also to Robin, Fox, and Great Lake too.

His attention was suddenly directed high in his branches toward Hawk's nest where another beginning was unfolding. The energy around him vibrated and shifted as the cosmic web continued its endless ebb and flow.

Gentle Breeze arrived, softly circling nest as it lay securely anchored in Tree's limbs. "I've come to gather news and witness Hawk's birth," he declared. Breeze then laughed as he looked upon Newborn Hawk and recognized an old friend.

"Welcome young one! Do you remember me? You have become Bird this day, but I knew you before when you lived as Snow on Mountain's peak."

Amused, Tree quipped, "Yes, and now born as Hawk she will not only journey alongside Cloud, but also be free to visit many snowy peaks."

"All true," Breeze chuckled. "Stream will enjoy this information." With a tender stroke against Hawk's wet feathers, Gentle Breeze continued on, for the forest was teeming with many stories to be both heard and conveyed.

It wasn't long before Newborn Hawk was joined by Fawn, Wildflower, Dragonfly, and Fern. Each taking first breaths, experiencing new forms with new purposes. Tree sighed happily, appreciating Mountain's changing scenery, and invited the lyrical vibrations of Earth's melodies to rise through his roots and find a home in his rings. And while Tree's leaves tilted upward, delighting in Sun's warm light and admiring Wren's songs, deep contentment filled his heart.

"This too shall pass..." Inner Voice spoke tenderly.

"Yes," Tree agreed, as his thoughts filled with stars and oceans, mountains and lakes. Each singing their ancient songs of light and dark, joy and sorrow. Together taking rhythmic breaths linking all things within a tapestry of endless life. "As is the way."

EPILOGUE
LEAF AND THE FIVE ELEMENTS: FIRE, EARTH, METAL, WATER, AND WOOD

THE STORY OF LEAF is rooted in my background as a Five Element acupuncturist and my desire to use the wisdom of nature and the Taoist philosophy of yin and yang to help my clients find their unique inner balance and achieve overall wellness.

The Five Elements are FIRE, EARTH, METAL, WATER, and WOOD. But they are much more than the literal components after which they are named. Within each element there is an energetic yin and yang movement, as well as a particular corresponding season, sound, emotion, color, direction, and more. Each element also offers gifts and strengths that may help empower us to better navigate through our inevitable struggles in life. On a daily basis, a person typically experiences a little of each element in some way or another. For example, we may laugh with a friend about an inside joke (fire), then plan and organize a presentation for school or work (wood), cook a delicious meal for our family (earth), sit quietly while looking out the window (water), or be inspired and moved by a poem (metal). Nature teaches us that change is inherently part of life. Thus, moving fluidly through each element without getting stuck is key to balanced health. The easier we embrace this universal truth, the better life will flow, giving us the opportunity to walk our paths with less resistance and more resilience.

Taoism is a Chinese philosophy that recognizes duality in the universe and encourages individuals to find harmony within nature's state of continual energetic flow and transformation. "The Tao" (Dao) is translated as "The Way," or more specifically, "the way of nature." The Taoist symbol of yin and yang represents the ongoing balance that constantly takes place in the natural world, and thus within us, too. The Chinese character for yang means "the bright side of a mountain," while yin is "the shady side of a mountain." Since the mountain is a complete entity, it holds both light and dark simultaneously.

Though considered opposites, each side is required to complete the whole, and therefore are actually dependent and complementary of each other. Yang energy is rising, sunny, hot, active and creative; Yin energy is sinking, dark, cold and receptive.

Chinese medicine uses yin and yang principles as a way to encourage health, both physically and emotionally. For example, if a body has too much rising heat (yang), a person may have cardiovascular issues, such as high blood pressure, or experience anxiety. Treatment would subsequently involve releasing that internal heat, and reinforcing the cooler yin energy to calm and soothe both body and mind.

Below describes the Five Elements and their corresponding yin and yang energetic flow, as well as each element's particular characteristics and how they are incorporated into *The Story of Leaf*:

FIRE: Leaf begins his story in the element of Fire, represented by the season of summer and the height of yang energy expression. The sound and emotion of Fire are laughter and joy, respectively, while its gifts include partnership, warmth, and passion. The energetic movement is one of rising and falling, like flames of a fire, which at times can be strong and billowing, or much less intense, like glowing embers. Building and maintaining healthy relationships among family and friends is an important component of this element. As Leaf enjoys summer on Mountain's sunny, or yang, side, he experiences a deep sense of comfort high in Tree surrounded by friends. Butterfly's visit and cheerful stories represents the rising energy and uplift we may feel after a good laugh and shared enjoyment. The feeling of joy, however, is always balanced in time with falling energy and periods of unhappiness. Squirrel's arrival and the sadness he experiences is an example of the emotional ups and downs we all go through. Allowing for the continual ebb and flow of emotions can help us avoid becoming overly stuck or worn down by them. In doing so, we are less hampered by periods of distress and better able to experience life with more ease and fluidity.

EARTH: Earth's season is represented by late summer, just after the height of summer has passed, yet the heat and humidity continue to hold on. The days, however, begin to shorten and the arrival of cooler weather is in the foreseeable future. This element has a circular energetic flow, allowing us to focus our thoughts and attention outward in order to nurture and care for others. Then, equally important, pulls nourishment back inward to provide for our own needs and growth. Leaf moves into the Earth element when he feels the dampness in the air, and sees the animals in the forest satisfying their hunger with the seasonal bounty of berries, fruit, and root vegetables. The sound associated with the element of Earth is "sing," while its corresponding gifts include service, transformation, sympathy, and thoughtfulness. Mother Robin embodies the qualities of Earth as she arrives to comfort Squirrel by singing to him. The strength of Earth is one's ability to remain centered and grounded while giving and receiving in proportionate measures. Earth teaches us the importance of empathy and compassion, and that finding and maintaining balance in one's life is the key to wellness.

METAL: Autumn represents Metal's season. As nature prepares for colder weather, the energy of yang is giving way and begins sinking and transforming into yin. This ability of "letting go" is a powerful component within this element. There is true freedom of flow when we let go of an item or long-held beliefs that no longer serve us. Saying goodbye to an old neighborhood and friends may be painful, but necessary for personal growth. Grief is the corresponding emotion of Metal, while the gifts include inspiration, acknowledgment, and respect. For example, Leaf is inspired by the colorful leaves surrounding him and in awe of Mountain's beauty, yet he experiences grief and the sense of loss when those same leaves around him fall off Tree. His grief intensifies even further when Wind carries him to the yin, or shaded, side of the Mountain. Metal's strength is the ability to find and appreciate the value in things, particularly when it's not obvious. Leaf's biggest lesson is learning to honor and respect his new location and letting go of previously held ideas that only the bright, yang side of the Mountain can bring him happiness.

WATER: The arrival of winter represents Water, along with the energetic expression of yin when it has reached its most dominant and robust stage. The time for rest, recuperation, and the storing of resources has arrived. Water's corresponding emotion is fear, while stillness, potency, wisdom, and the ability to listen are Water's gifts. Leaf is upset when he first arrives at Brother Fox's den because he is fearful of its quiet darkness, not yet understanding those exact conditions will finally allow him to witness Mountain's life and hear its message. Water teaches us to be still and listen, giving us the opportunity for peaceful introspection and a chance to hear our inner wisdom. The energetic flow of this element is considered deep, and honors water's natural inclination to follow a downward slope of least resistance. Water's power, however, is in its ability to keep going, even when obstacles are in the way, and not give up while reaching for one's potential.

WOOD: The energetic resources that were gathered and stored during the colder months are now ready to burst forward with direction and purpose, like an arrow released from its bow flying toward its intended goal. Spring is the season of the Wood element, while birth, creation, vision, and clarity are its gifts. The energetic movement of Wood is up and out, mirroring a young green sprout growing up and spreading out in order to harness the sun's warmth and life-giving light. After Leaf became Water and spent restorative yin time with Great Lake, he feels a strong urge to keep moving and thus enters Stream to continue his journey. Yin is now releasing its hold and transforming into yang, which enthusiastically resumes its natural rising momentum. Spring in the forest has arrived and the powerful pulse of creation is eager to express itself. Leaf, as Water, finally finds the roots he was seeking and emerges as a strong and vibrant tree. Wood teaches us the power of vision and direction, as well as our abilities to set goals and carry them out to completion.